Turkish Delight
A Kid's Guide To Istanbul, Turkey

Photography By John D. Weigand
Poetry By Penelope Dyan

Bellissima Publishing, LLC
Jamul, California
www.bellissimapublishing.com

ISBN 978-1-935630-54-8

First Edition

To times long past...
And to things that last.

Turkish Delight

Bellissima Publishing, LLC

Introduction

What a surprise to go to Istanbul, Turkey and to see all the wonderful things that a kid can see. If you can't go in person, then travel along with author Penelope Dyan and photographer, John D. Weigand and see Istanbul, Turkey through their eyes. Feel free to add to this book and make notes and add tickets and postcards inside, or other things that you may find in Istanbul when you go there. See how many of these sights and things you can find, and be sure to look for even more on your journey there.

The whole idea of all of the Dyan/Weigand travel books is to let you see some of the things kids might like to see when they travel to other countries, and to give you a real taste and flavor of these places. These books with the poetry of Penelope Dyan and the photographs of John D. Weigand are different from any other kids' travel books out there, because they are meant to stir the imaginations of children, not to spoon feed them facts that are boring and easy to forget. Children remember what catches their eyes.

Penelope Dyan is a former teacher, an attorney and an award winning writer. Two of her books for children have been chosen by the UK Arts Council and are on display at the Saisoon Poetry library on the fifth floor of the Royal Exhibit Hall at Southbank Centre, London,. Two of her other books are listed in the best books (top ten) on the Pukeke Reading list in Australia, and her book "Surfer Girl" was best teen book at both the 2008 New York Book Festival and the 2008 Hollywood Book Festival and is also recognized on the Girls' Voices In Literature Database, Miami University Florida.

Turkish Delight

Bellissima Publishing, LLC

Turkish Delight
A Kid's Guide To Istanbul, Turkey

Photography By John D. Weigand
Poetry By Penelope Dyan

Istanbul is an exciting and colorful city,
that is very interesting and very pretty.
Buildings and mosques reach up to the skies,
and so many things will catch your eyes.

You can stay in a small, quaint hotel,
near where the Turkish people shop and dwell.
The Blue Mosque and Santa Sophia Church
are a short distance away,
(from this location) if you decide to stay.

You can walk to shop at the Grand Bazaar,
Because, after all, it isn't too far.

There are shops there with all kinds of things, even emeralds and rubies and diamond rings!

You can take a walk to the Blue Mosque as well. (It has lots of blue in it and stories to tell.)

And you can walk to the Arasta Bazaar.
It's open on Sunday, and it isn't too far.

You can buy pitchers and coffee pots,
and baskets and things!
You can find bracelets and bangles,
and so many things!

You can find great shoes for kids,
that you can wear on your feet.
You will feel like you are walking on air
as you walk down the street!
And all of these shoes are made by hand,
by an expert shoe maker in this far away land.

And just look at the hand made felt hats,
and the felt balls in THIS store!
And as you walk along happily
you can see EVEN MORE!

Outside a restaurant I saw these fish,
waiting to be cooked, and to be put on a dish!

At Santa Sophia time has come to a stop,
from the roots of its foundations,
way up to its top.

Take a look at the beauty and majesty inside,
that even new added artifacts just cannot hide.

See the Angel Gabriel mosaic
between the pillars strong.
You can almost hear Gabriel's song.

And a short walk away see the cistern deep,
where ancient Roman's their water did keep.

And at the end of the cistern,
(standing on her head)
is the likeness of Medusa
that the ancients did dread.
Don't look into her eyes!
Don't go there alone!
Or you may find
YOU are turned into stone!

There are Roman aqueducts,
that once brought water from Bulgaria
to this ancient city. . .

And here I am outside Santa Sophia saying good-bye to a small kitty.

"ADIEU! I HAVE TOO GRIEVED A HEART
TO TAKE A TEDIOUS LEAVE."
William Shakespeare

JUL 2 9 2014

CPSIA information can be obtained
at www.ICGtesting.com
Printed in the USA
LVIW012322080512
280960LV00002B